MW01279995

RE – EVOLUTION

HALA DIKA

Wasteland Press
Shelbyville, KY USA
www.wastelandpress.net

Re-Evolution
By Hala Dika

First Printing—January 2010
ISBN: 978-1-60047-392-0

Printed in the U.S.A.

Contents

Reborn

A darkness beyond repair moved like a wolf inside. Now ordained, I let it come. Born again, God slapped my face and taught me how to scream. Rays of light gathered around my waist and lifted me toward Heaven. The streets I roamed, with Love and Death. I slept on benches, lived on tomatoes, and played a tune for a buck.

In the New World there is only the clarity of the beating heart and the unbeating heart, the soul, absolute navigator, all directions equal in prospect, the sun and the moon. The slummer is bound by no man, re-inventing everything.

I have no use for reality. There is no better world than my own. I wish to conquer no other.

I am no coward, though I am shy. I smile a lot, no reason why. I'll talk to you if you try. Lets go somewhere and get high, you talk and I'll cry.

Every lamppost has a rule, don't park, don't eat, don't cough, don't drool. What does everybody say? We need more rules for happier days. Why aren't you happy, I would ask? We need more money, need more cash. What a very peculiar bunch, watch them gorging down their lunch!

Where are you? My mysterious cutout lover. What body will you take to give to me? But tell me about your eyes dear lover, what will they see? I am periling, please hurry!

There is no meaning after this, some call it Hell, others, bliss. What have I said that you will take, in your imaginations re-make? A world of nonsense that is mine, has served me well through this and thine!

Nuclear Poets

Poetry is too pretty a word for the ugly work of the poet.
It is not an extraordinary life,
One begins by asking for nothing and receiving little,
We are fools, but of a Shakespearian nature,
Too wise for our own good, too happy, too sad,
Rotten at conversation,
Our minds wander within the space of a second,
Inspired by God knows what!
Ill-equipped, ill-fitted, undesirable, and permanently marked,
Like a fire, others enjoy, refusing to get too close,
Incapable of the approved normalcy,
Too stupid to fake it,
When finally we speak,
We are sorry we bothered,
Ungratified, restless, we walk the streets in search of answers,
All we find is more pain,
Often,
Things still manage to look alive,
But most times they are indescribably marred,
We take in the world and return to our lonely rooms,
Thinking,
Human beings are a disgrace!
Would rather shoot you than shake your hand,
Caught up in the dirty stew of nationalism, patriotism, the one
true God,
Beyond that, they split into infinitudes,
Each time, justifying the Atom.

The Nuclear Age!
And a nuclear poet!
Splicing atoms with words,
That is what I'll be from now on,
Since holding a bomb is the only way of being heard!

On the Cleanliness of Dirt

Cleanliness is not next to Godliness,
The worst people are clean-shaven,
Armies reek of disinfectant before taking their bloodbath.

The day belongs to the market,
Insatiable animal!
Like a fat child who is never full.
In the gutter,
All activity is ominous,
Laughter issues from the mouths of the dead,
Taking malignant pride in misfortune,
Angels confess love to demons.

Impossible to move every soul,
Backfire.
People are like stubborn children,
They only comprehend absence,
Playing catch-up with my time.

Vision and Solitude,
Curse and Creation,
Love is for the child-people.

Another Sermon!

Here I sit,
Waiting for God to drop a brick
From the heavens,
At maximum speed,
It should readily awaken understanding.

And so my poems should be,
Of this century,
Dropped from on-high
Or perhaps from the stratosphere,
Our sleep being so deep!

Are there many good jokes in the Bible?
You have to read between the lines,
God is funny,
But only in depth,
The devil is funny,
But base.

We are living with an in-between God.

People say balance.
Balance in Nature
Balance in Man,
But I see nothing so balanced.
Beneath our proprietary cloak,
We are either more angel,
Or more demon,
And it is not our duty, which makes us thus,
But our faith,

And the cell is within our own minds,
Latched with a golden bolt and a silver handle,
Deeply cut in DENIAL
We are warden and prisoner alike.

It is easier to kiss a stranger,
Than a potential lover,
Love does not stand on ceremony.

Do you wonder at the sanctity of objects?

Cigars are smoked vanity.

The Rich think they know,
The poor are certain,
But suffering alone does not crystallize virtue
A human-being,
Will all the frailties
And none of the humanity,
Like an aristocrat,
With all the nobility,
And none of the majesty.

We abhor blasphemy,
Yet are content to judge for God,
To wield the mighty gavel.

So much talk and nothing to say,
Wise ones die,
While wicked ones pray.

Remember your inequities,
Before you give claim to self-pity,
This is a sobering device.

Fungus never grows on a poor man's bread,
Only the gluttonous produce mold,
So much so,
My stomach turns at it!

I've heard that miners have a double religion,
Praise God on the outside,
And Satan in the mines,
The priest cannot convince them otherwise,

Though he is not susceptible to falling sky,
And when the children emerge,
Caked in dust,
It is surely from Hell they've come,
And the Devil who spares them till dawn.

Testing...Testing

Dreams lag into dawn and haunt my day with their apparitions
I am the perpetual pillow-maker,
Dreaming all day long,
You will find me on rooftops in the spring,
On bridges in the winter,
Making of my day, a paradise,
Skipping to some silly tune,
Wandering like a pleased buffoon,
Happy with myself,

In my solitary room,
I contend with demons,
As they come one by one,
To disturb my slumber,
How clever they are to wait until the dead of night,
To show me their black and feathered nightingale,
Which they perch on my window,
To carry some pain with her mournful song,
Will I ever be free of these snaky devils!

I am a fool
As we all are,
Living,
Breathing,
Fools,
How we allow the God-given day,
To be swallowed up by numb propriety,
How we sell our most precious gifts to the highest bidder,
To drink champagne,
And snort cocaine,
And die in a rusty old bathroom.

In order to live,
I condemn myself to death,
The surest way to find joy,
Is to know that there is nothing left to feel,

To discover that life is a spiritual journey,
And the body,
A mere obstacle,
To be stripped bare and rebuilt.

There is no definitive "good life",
There is no way a human being may reach this paradise,
Some are content in the life of family, church, pub,
I am not,
And since I,
As well as anyone else has not seen Heaven,
I tear myself apart to find it in all things living, breathing, alive,
I once took this measure to extremes and was graciously
rewarded,
Only to find that the final step was a gateway through Hell,
Perhaps this is the reason that men prefer the ordinary and would
rather not know,
But we cannot escape that earth is Heaven and Hell combined,
The Atom bomb nestled between the devils criss-crossed legs.

When I finally realized I could not run,
I stood to face,
I had never seen such a Sun,
Such a Sky,
All things were sweating and breathing and the wind was like
fire!
I had returned to the desert,
Figures in the distance seemed to rise from the hot cement like
white flames,
Quivering to rhythms in my head,
If I was listening to jazz,
Their dance would be achingly connected to God,
And all those things he was filling my head with,
My soul growing too large for my body,
I took in the world with smiles and silences.

Sleep may rob you of midnight ambitions,
And leave you wondering what you ever thought of yourself,
Yes,
Sleep is the reapers favorite charm,
He dangles it in front of you to lull you into death.
In the morning we kick ourselves out of the grave and pour cold
water on our faces,
And forget last night's noble ambitions.
But we cannot deny that irresistible pull back to our coffin.
Dracula was merely a night crawler,
His eyes attune to darker things,
A hopeless,
Blood-sucking,
Romantic.

Army Oath

Here come the Generals,
Woop dee dee,
Bow your heads and hold your pee,
Come yon lads from every hill,
In the army you will thrill,
To spill your blood,
And spill blood still.

My Mind It Lives

My mind it lives on fantasy,
Illusions are its prey,
It sees just what it wants to see,
Protects itself from day,
And in this imagined state,
Lets imagination play.

My mind it works prolifically,
A prisoner to my soul,
It rants and raves inside its shell,
Like termites in a bowl,
And forsakes reason for a dream,
It will not be controlled.

It watches as the workers pass,
And does not wish to join,
The world it whirls around its head,
Its fate tossed like a coin,
Today it lives in New York City,
Tomorrow in De Moine!

"You must secure a good position,"
The rationalist may say,
"You must depend upon your class,
And never go astray!"

Let "good position" rot in Hell,
My mind I live today!

Free-Fall

Rhythms jumpin, high-energy masquerade,
Light penetrating everything, dancing on shingles and brows,
Hummin a tune I know,
Miles on the player turning to night beats,
Beatniks in coffee shops in black berets spew smoke-filled words
with jazzy refrains,

Lead me far away where things escape, cloaked in black silk,
And silent whispers of after-thoughts swingin in the rain,
Here comes the man all dressed in blue,
Handing out tickets to me and you,
Glassy eyes and false rebukes.

Suicide on my mind,
Sits in the back, pulls up a heart-attack and smokes a sack,
Of Lucky Strikes in paper wraps.

From the corner of my eye death laughs,
Rattles her whiskey glass,
Ice-filled,
A chill,
Blows through freezes my will,
Take a pill.
Don't call me in the morning when my day isn't sworn in,
And all I have yet to be is torn,
In the first appearance of blue.

My eyes ride high, look east and west,
No sense of freedom, a gasp for breath,
Night may linger, leavin me in cold sweats,
Depressed, a mess, no signs of outer-success.

Drinking alone on the second floor,
I explore all that is unsure,
Invent the sickness and disdain the cure.

The Shingles

For Poe

I

Hear the clamor of the shingles-
Hollow shingles!
When they shiver and they twinkle!
How they tingle, tingle, tingle
Down the ladder of my spine!
In sweet echoes, how they mingle,
While the moon, solemn and single,
In the darkness is entwined,
As they dance, dance, dance,
In a symphony of romance,
To a windy hymn they jingle,
Oh the shingles, shingles, shingles,
Shingles, shingles, shingles-
Oh the tingling and the mingling of the shingles.

II

Hear the rhythm of the shingles-
Silvery shingles!
What a world of mystery in their light and airy jingle!
Through the eddies of the air,
What a magic they prepare!-
From their intermittent song,
So possessed by the breeze,
How they seem to get along,
With the moon who bends an ear,
Round and yellow through the trees!
Oh, the eyes of children twinkle,
At the melody they sprinkle!
How they jingle!
How they tingle,
In the moment they out-single,

Through a vast deserted dingle,
Oh the timing and the chiming,
Of the shingles, shingles, shingles-
To the clamor thus enamored by the shingles!

Wise Woman

I weep for all pains,
There is no creature ignored by me,
In the tradition of my ancestors,
Nightmares are fulfilled in the day,
And cast away like demons,
Who cannot exist in the sun,.
Headaches are cured with bare hands,
And soft prayers,
I bear the faith which knows no end.

Winter

I see only white,
Stars out of sight,
The moon in its realm is silenced.
In the distance a white cross,

JESUS
A
V
E
S

Dream

They slowly walked off the bus,
Skinny, rod-like bodies,
Structures of gray sand,
Crumbling.
Their legs barely fit into their shoes,
They left behind pieces of themselves
An arm or leg,
A shoulder,
A spine,
The bus was shrouded in their gray frames.
They walked back to where they came from,
Shadows of living forms.
The white man watched through his binoculars,
Satisfied in the knowledge that it was *he*,
Who had allowed them to get out alive.

Warlock Soup Song

Farcical passage,
Allochthonous Fate
Sun through the citadel,
Stoic mass servitude,
Giving way to oblivion,
In the searching of the Stone.

Funeral

How the living love to honor the dead,
Good deeds are less shameful in the grave,
And people will exalt your name,
Who spoke little of you while you lived,

And family will gather and weep,
And mother will be dragged from the pit,
Faint and fall into a maddening fit,
And father will break things,
As he often did,

And brother will take it all to heart,
For shame I should play such a part!
So I suppose suicide is out of the question,
The most I'll get is an honorable mention!

Heathens' Blood

Do wa, do wa, do wa ditty,
The years roll by in this dark city.
Wake to see the sun go down,
The young turn old,
The leaves turn brown,
And still we march or walk or run,
To mindless jobs, devoid of Sun.
The cry for war,
More War!
More War!
Let's kill and kill!
Will we ever have our fill?
Of bodies piled to the sky,
Of mother's scream,
And father's cry.

The little politician's hat,
Is worn by a short and ugly man,
Who could not count to 1, 2, 3,
Had not his nanny laid the plan.
And still, "Home Team!"
We roar and roar,
And let the flags and banners soar,
Till round our ankles comes the flood,
Of victory drenched in heathens' blood.

In-Patient

The only equality is in madness,
Insanity is a potent leveler,
The meaning of life is in the living,
Defying any singular explanation.
The value of freedom is possessed solely by the
Incarcerated.
Love's had me committed twice,
With a handshake and smile.

1

My soul is in the desert,
Among the incalculable vastness
All figures rising from the sands,
Between life and eternity,
Where reigns the kingdom of silences,
Of which I am queen.

My heart is a desert,
Of which love enters liberally,
Each love is new,
Alive with its own beauty,
Cursed in its own special way,
I believed I could win in absentia,
But I find it a futile effort,
Hope,
A fearsome prospect,
Tell me,
Who will love a warrior woman.

A Minute In

The children awake playing a trumpet,
While my fingers grapple under a heavy stone tomb,
Slowly wrap around the inch between the darkness and light,
Blinded by the sliver of sun,
My bladder forces me out.

The coffee burns my tongue,
And cigarettes help my breathe,
The modern Buddhist meditates with nicotine.

What is modern if not Rubbermaid?

The poet of tomorrow is an ancient thinker,
Carving simple truths on stone tablets,
Too heavy to send out,
Alabaster conversations with God,

Steal the morning when you can,
And happiness when it isn't looking,

Love just kicked me in the gut,
And with my dying breath,
I ask her to do it again.

Never Say Die

Never say die. The spirits are strong and the mind belligerent. The heart will dance the ladder of notes and when the music stops, to the butterfly. Sun in, Sun out. Why? Because it is. Why tire ourselves with questioning? What does it matter? And the Great Mother says here is rain and sky and love and love and love. Bring down your fantasies unto the earth and fight with your bare feet on the warm cement. And though the whole world be watching, there are none but two. And dust to dust and ash to ash, a day, a year, an hour. What actions your feet take, your heart to break and mine. And though the signs be overwhelming, do not make the transformation alone, for I too am changing though still a bag of blood and veins and bone.

So mania they call it. I call it life. I did not beat my fists to blood to be imprisoned by freedom. There can be sorrow under the sun as there is joy under the moon, and the stars, speaking silence. You see! It rains under the bright light!

I speak to you in poetry because we have never been formally introduced. Because we are yet familiar. This is something. I know where you go. We meet in *the Drifting*. Music is dream. What is real? Life is dream. What is true? Dream is real. We decide. We are the word and the word is action. If they call us dreamers, it is only because their reality is flawed. And what joy should I find in their belated understanding when it has been apparent, born in me? And loneliness born along. But why complain, great sorrows, profound joys. Follow me! I will show you!!! Do not trust my skin, I am quite old, wrinkling my soul with living and love. What other purpose should the *real world* hold? I'll bide my time in loving arms, sings songs, and drink wine.

Ballad of Futility

So begins the death of feeling,
No desire except the desire for solitude,
An end to talk!
Ever tried to be alone while someone was in the room,
No desire to change things,
No desire to be loved,
No desire to be needed,
No desire,
Nothing,
A peaceful hole,
Nothing to be gained from life,
Nothing to be gained from death,
A nuclear explosion,
Millions of bodies burned to a crisp all around me,
And me,
Standing there,
Stoic,
With my cup of coffee and my cigarette.

Dreamicide

What maddens the soul,
Is the miniscule thinking,
Which stifles the genesis,
Of an unusually prolific idea,
An idea to save lives,
And sets it to stretching,
Against the metallic gears of bureaucracy,
Depressing the very essence of justice,
In a dull persistence for claims,
Killing the dream,
And though it rise again,
We will lose *the dreamer.*

Firecracker

The redcoats have come and gone,
So the bluecoats fashioned a different throne,
Every man, woman, child has the right to be free,
A seeming statement of the deepest clarity,
Land of the free, home of the brave,
Ploughed and flowered by the hands of the slave,
A thousand lashes to the one who sought to read,
Lest he discover he too should be freed,
So the white man came first,
And the black man last,
The Indians cleansed,
So the die was cast,
Independence achieved through blood, sweat, and tears,
Democracy rooted,
In deep-seeded fears,
Now the hate is well cushioned,
By the way it is said,
Still it hardly takes a minute,
To go from orange to red.

Happy

Here's a tip from someone who knows
When you're happy, don't think.
Just feel,
It is a stolen moment.

Humdinger

So many gifts, so little time,
As the clock winds,
Down and our dreams unrealized,
To shit,
Quit?
Me? Never!
Down in the dumps,
Up in the clouds,
Breathe the sweet air of paradise,
Take the final breath,
Dead is the end,
Of it,
So it goes.
Down under,
Beneath the rolling thunder,
Never to return,
Let the wheel of sorrow burn,
I will rise again from rivers of ash and,
Take my place at the head of the table,
Break bread and prepare to bleed.

If Only the Struggle

I sometimes think it would content me if I never spoke again. For so often the vocalization of sentiment results in a cheapening of spirit and the depth of a comprehending silence is shattered by some idiot phrase or social convention, which ends in hypocrisy. The only words I spew with ease, "coffee, regular, two sugars please!"

What human beans struggle to correct are their own horrible creations. But why waste time rebelling against a race I should leave behind. The locusts are descending and no doorway escapes blood. Alas! There is nowhere left to hide. Goddamned satellites! Goddamned discovery! Goddamn everything created by man!

There must be one good thing, you say. But what? I am as anxious as you to admit something. Name me one thing that has not caused destruction, I implore you! But then again without destruction perhaps we would not need poets at all. So the very thing we attempt to alter has given us rise!

What is it that we want? Something that has never existed, a state of universal tolerance and love, but not the kind of tolerance required by law, something much deeper, a genuine understanding that we would all gain from such efforts. Every individual taking responsibility for the race, and so we may finally begin to recognize the soul of every man on this earth, to aspire to the highest and most noble calling of man, love, charity without demand for recognition, fame, or money, to stop depending on Heaven for that final consolation, procrastinating paradise in favour of all the weaknesses God has placed on our heads. Defy such a God that would deem us so damned predictable!

Impression

One must never come to it the way others perceive it,
But rather the way it *is*.

Love is Death

How much patience can I have?
I wish and I wait,
The demon rebel feeds off pride,
Say, give up,
But I don't have the energy to start over,
I have your scent now,
And I taste it in the most obscure places,
Like a distilled memory,
The child inside betrays my warrior pose,
I am tired of fighting
Come die with me awhile.

Never in Vain

Mothers would rather they bore no prophets,
Mothers would keep their children safe,
Silence them for their protection,
But God will not be silenced,
He will take the child and teach it resistance,
And the subtleties of grace,
Then send him out into the world,
Among the sharks
To speak the truth,
Innocent blood,
To be hurt,
Ridiculed,
Rejected,
Sacrificed,
Committed,

And mother can do nothing but watch,
For the child is bold,
For the child is proud,
He speaks and the people listen,

Soon the state is summoned,
Mother begs and asks why?
Prophesizes the outcome,
The child will die,

And what can Mary do?
But kneel and weep,
But one day soon she will realize,
The child died not in vain,
For another prophet from his heels,
Will take up the reigns again!

Mad Summer

I dare not feel happiness and the words today come only when the music plays. To be hated is of no consequence. In the outer hallway the sounds of life play as mother and child. I get ahead of myself. See the prize with all its glory, I have no patience. I tend to see it, know it and move on.

I hate myself. There! Let me put it out there for you reader, because I believe you hate yourself too. If you say no, pardon my French but you are a fucking liar!

I have an orange glass and a head of light fairy spirits, they dance around and around. Do with me what you will, devils, angels. Pluck my strings or spit in my face, sing songs.

Philanthropists Wake

Clay figures,
Breathe life onto yourselves when the maker is absent,

Marionettes,
String yourselves along when the puppetmaster's gone,

For though you pray five times a day,
Your wishes are by deeds granted,

And the light can be seen before the final passing,
So the path is well-lit
Only marred by greed,

A sum on every head,
A tag on every soul,
Nothing is priceless,
The truth an apology
War over the shelf,

So do not sink prayers in wishing wells,
Barter with Heaven,
While courting in Hell.

Tourist

Miserable creatures,
Maintaining lies,
To keep the chickens from pecking,
Amputating perfectly good limbs,
White-washing that one black spot,
Carving out the heart of you,
The soul of you,
Traveling across continents,
Encapsulated in your province,
Refusing water,
Entirely aware,
You have already been contaminated!

Respect

Pity is almost a form of hate,
I would never want to be pitied,
I *prefer* to be hated.

Second Chance

Four walls and the door was locked, the world outside was stifled, claustrophobia rampant. Running through my head, thoughts of escape. Other men put up these walls, men who did not know me, love me. I'd become a burden to society, a patient.

The nurse came in, I did not know her, I did not know my own mother, I could have sworn I was free. She gave me pudding. I spit in her face. Had I ever been so direct? So honest? So impolite?

Doctors entered in blurred figures of white and blue and shining of silver. They were all alike, all of them.

Dreams came of all kinds, me on a stretch-cart being rolled toward the light by angels in doctor suits. They'd roll me toward a door and the dream would be over.

I collected all the guitars in the hospital, but I did not play them.

They put plasma on my temples; they pumped serum through my veins. The vapor burned my lungs and took me away. I was not there when they pulled the switch. I wonder if my body wriggled like a jellyfish, like I've seen in the movies. I felt like a scrambled television being kicked to work.

And then I was awake. And there was my mother and the nurses and doctors staring over me. And then there were the others, people like me who shared a secret, a world outside a world.
"Hi, I'm fucked, you?"
"Yeah."
"Nice to meet you!"

Bridgette was my roommate, a 35-year-old lesbian. One girl spent all her time drawing, one dude playing ping-pong. A hip old broad named Rosie would spontaneously rise from her wheelchair and do the twist! Wild man!

Forgot most of their names, because I tried to forget. I was wrong. One should never forget, for these people co-existed during a discovery.

I find pain is not something I seek, but it will come. It will come in all forms; it will even disguise itself as happiness.

Who knows why it all happened? But it did.

Simile

Innocence is like a child ballerina,
Pirouetting into smoke.

Stone-Sober

You are a fighter,
That's what you are,
You rise to the challenge,
And fall into the depths,
Swim the sewers,
Taste the shit,
Wade in the excess,
Till your face is black
Crawl up the landslide
An inch above,
A foot below,
Never rewarded.

You shout at the people,
Look!
See!
And they shun you for it.
All hail the poet!
All hail the poet!

You give your love without return
Laughter, your dearest gift!
You stay too long,
To keep from being alone,
And oh! The people you meet!
You drifter,
You loner,
You goalless crusader!

Alone, you take it on,
And most times that's peaceful,
And most times that's pleasurable, preferable even!
No masks to put on,
No courtesies to uphold,
No fashions to obey.

Fantasy,
She knows how to pass the time,
Reality,
She knows how to make you hard,
Rough,
Buried,
Belittled.

A proper cynic!
She latches on to the sweet-stoned dawn,
While you're walkin,
And the birds seem to fly in your name,
Their wings a masterpiece,
"Wish you had wings,
Wish you had wings,"
They seem to tease,
In the mysterious, incoherent art of chirping,

They sense your heartache,
But deny it as such.
I've suffered, I say,
Fly! They say,
It's too painful, I say,
Fly! They say,
I want to die,
Fly! Fly! Fly!
Is their incessant reply.

The Jest

Manic clowns are doing a roundabout dance in my head,
Neurotic, with mouths of black,
The emptiness running down their throats,
Wide open,
Screaming soundless fury,
Maniacal laughter at my expense,
You idiotic humans!
They sing,
Take this illusion life too seriously,
Die a little and dance a lot,
Until you too are crazy enough to understand,
That happiness and madness are of the same sweet cup,
Spin yourself into delirium,
And fall heavy upon your bed,
The dawn is not new,
And life is one long day.

Too Late

The coward smirks in the face of truth,
He will wear that smirk to his grave,
And then,
There,
On his final death rattle,
He will lose it.

Up

Strange the desires of men,
Strange their needs,
Their wants,
Run away little birds,
With your innocent flight home,
If I were a little bird,
Where would I not roam,
The heavens surmountable?
I would linger on the shoulders of angels,
Hob-knob with the saints,
Ask God to forgive the Devil,
So we all know paradise.

Who You Know

Those who fear to speak the truth,
For fear of offending the minions of the bitch-goddess success,
Are dead already,
And their works will die with them,
For they will not be around to kiss ass eternally!

A Despairing God

What a fine mess!
Evolution on the skids!
Someone put a wrench in it!
DNA is done for!
It were better we accept our fate as animals,
With territory, fear, hunger, and more territory!
Hope is a dull word, a naïveté,
Love, Exterminated.

Great Minds

When I squint my eyes,
The words are like armies of ants,
Threatening to march off the page,
Faces appear from spaces,
Millions of little blues canoes,
Carrying a message,
Each with a poem to deliver,
All headed,
In perfect form,
In the same direction.

Re-Evolution

Paradise is a place in preconception
The nothingness that exists before our life in the womb,
Not emptiness, I say, but nothingness,
For emptiness requires life and experience, memory, and regret,
The knowledge that once there was a fullness that is no longer
present,
Preconception is a blessing.

But then we are born,
And that first taste of cold air and oxygen makes us scream and
shiver in absolute terror,
Placed in the arms of the mother,
Our need for love begins.
Forever hence this need will cause joy and pain,
A never-ending struggle,
Laughter, tears, self-contempt, shame,
Our blood rising and falling like the tides,
In accordance with Sun and Moon,
Neither being grasped for too long.
We only suffer when we attempt to capture any single emotion.
There is no always,
And there never will be.
Happiness, despair,
No two moods can encapsulate the human soul,
It is a million Gods and contradictions,
Child, invalid, criminal, lover, prophet,
All at once,
As the tightrope walker,
We are balancing without a net.
A bird has more sense,
It eats, sleeps, flies north, flies south,
But we are victims of emotion,
And can as easily hate as love,
Kill as hug.

When we are good.
We tire of being heroes,
Because good deeds go unrecognized,
Or breed contempt from the very ones we offer them to,
We turn back to our defenses again and again,
In masochistic fashion,
War within as well as without.

It is even more difficult to change the mentality of the angry
horde,
Who have increased their hate by numbers,
Taken up symbols with flags and fire,
One brain.

War offers simple-minded solutions,
A swift act of annihilation,
But peace,
There is the true struggle,
Acceptance of your neighbor is one hell of a fight!
The atom bomb is a one-button solution,
Love takes guts.

It is assumed that men play God by displaying the ability to kill,
But perhaps that has always been a human trait.
It is far more dangerous to free men,
To provide sanctuary,
Men of power have always feared the emergence of an actual
saint,
They would snuff them out as quickly as an insect,
Whose bussing outweighs their lies.

Human beings are feeble when it comes to compassion,
They must constantly be reminded,
Left alone for a moment,
And they segregate on the substance of a single black spot.
I imagine God to be a very disgusted figure.
I dare not make a single demand,
Or sink so low as to place blame.
But tell me,

Will the guilty be smitten?
If they cannot perceive of damnation,
How can they be damned?
When will the meek inherit?
What defines meekness?
Good?
Why would God equate justice with weakness?
Does he not then equate strength with brutality?
What hope have we, if this is the case?
There is something fundamentally wrong with the whole
equation.

It is nothing less than maddening to assume any one solution,
A single answer devolves into a thousand questions,
And then we are right back where we started,
Hairy and dumbstruck by the creation of fire,
The first technological upset,
Out of the Dark Ages,

And yet to see the light.

We roam this earth blind as bats,
Scratching and clawing to exist,
Masquerading our every intention with a polite word,
Though sincerity is never so polite.
We are asleep, subdued, medicated,
And to think,
We pity the lab rat,
Pity yourselves with the larger brain!

There are so many things to conceal the truth,
Gadgets, gizmos, entertainments of all kinds,
In Time Square tourists take pictures of pictures!
With so much wool over our eyes,
I wonder if we ever will see,
I assure you,
It is easier not to,
But what is infinitely worse is to see,
And ignore our own certainty,

Like faces without mouths,
Mouths without tongues,
Bodies without spirit.
In this way,
Though we are created in God's image,
We die,
Soulless,
Without dignity or faith.

It is not enough to shed tears in the darkness of the movie house,
True belief is not an hour's worth,
But a lifetime,
A faith to surpass the grave,
Long after the body is devoured by very indifferent worms.

Death is kinder to those who do not fear it,
Do not join in with the million self-pitying fools,
Who say, "I am only human,"
Rather strive to be more
Never cage the lion,
Dark powers tend to implode upon themselves,
In due course,
But only if we rise to the occasion.

CPSIA information can be obtained at www.ICGtesting.com
Printed in the USA
BVOW030521180613

323144BV00012B/36/P